UPGRADE YOUR BRAIN WITH AI

Real Scenarios. Real Prompts. Real Results.

DINESH MANOHARAN

notionpress.com

INDIA • SINGAPORE • MALAYSIA

ISBN
Paperback 979-8-90479-573-3
Hardcase 979-8-90479-825-3

DISCLAIMER: The information contained in this book is intended for educational purposes only. The author and publisher are not responsible for any misuse of the techniques described. AI tools, their pricing, features, and capabilities change rapidly; readers are encouraged to verify current details on each provider's official website before making business decisions. Examples involving cybersecurity are intended to help defenders, IT professionals, and learners. Readers must follow their organization's policies, applicable laws, and professional ethics when applying these techniques.

ATTRIBUTION OF SOURCES: Where references, frameworks, statistics, or third-party materials are used, attribution is provided either inline or in the References section at the end of the book. If you believe any attribution is missing or incorrect, please reach out so it can be corrected in future editions.

Dedication

To every learner who refuses to be left behind, to every working professional who finishes the day tired but still opens one more tab to learn something new, and to every team that wants to do better work without burning out: this book is for you.

To my family, mentors, colleagues, and the security and IT communities whose questions over coffee, on calls, and in late-night chat threads shaped the scenarios in these chapters: thank you.

Contents

Foreword

There is a quiet revolution happening at desks, in server rooms, in classrooms, and in cafeterias around the world. People who once spent hours wrestling with the same recurring tasks, drafting the same kinds of emails, summarizing the same meetings, writing the same scripts, are quietly finishing them in minutes. They look the same on the outside. The difference is invisible: they have learned how to think with an AI assistant by their side.

This book is not about hype. It is not about replacing humans, and it is not about the latest viral demo. It is about something much more practical and much more useful: how to take the AI tools that already exist, the ones you can sign up for in five minutes, and use them to do your real work better. Whether you are a college student trying to prepare for placements, a junior systems engineer chasing tickets, a security analyst triaging alerts at two in the morning, a marketing executive preparing a campaign deck, or a senior manager trying to see the wood for the trees, the same set of skills will quietly transform how you work.

What you will find in these pages is the result of countless real-world conversations, prompt experiments, post-incident reviews, study sessions, and code reviews where AI assistants made a measurable difference. The book covers ChatGPT, Google Gemini, Anthropic Claude, xAI Grok, and Google NotebookLM. It does not pretend any of them is perfect, and it does not pretend any of them is dangerous magic. It treats them as what they are: powerful tools that reward thoughtful users and disappoint lazy ones.

Read this book with a notebook open and one of these AI tools loaded in another tab. Try every prompt. Adapt them to your own work. Push back when the answer looks wrong. Ask follow-up questions. Most of all, treat the AI as a tireless junior collaborator: helpful, fast, sometimes confidently mistaken, always willing to revise. That mindset alone will set you apart.

The world is not going to slow down to wait for any of us. But with the right habits and the right prompts, you can move faster without burning out. That is the promise of this book.

Preface: Why This Book Exists

This book exists because of a pattern I kept seeing. In every industry I visited, in every team I worked with, the same scene repeated itself. A few people on the team had quietly become two or three times more productive because they had learned to use AI assistants well. The rest of the team either had not tried, had tried once and given up, or were using these tools in such shallow ways that they were getting almost no benefit.

The gap between these two groups was not intelligence. It was not seniority. It was not even how technical they were. The gap was practice with prompts, and a clear mental model of what each tool is good at. That gap is closeable in a weekend, if you have the right examples in front of you. Unfortunately, most articles online either gush over AI in vague terms or drown the reader in technical jargon. Very few show, in plain language, what to type, what to expect back, and what to do with the result.

That is the gap this book tries to close. Every chapter is built around scenarios you will recognize from your own working life. Every scenario comes with prompts you can copy, adapt, and use today. Every chapter ends with practice exercises so you can build muscle memory rather than just nod along.

Who This Book Is For

This book is written for a wide audience because the underlying skill, learning to think clearly with an AI assistant, is universal. Specifically, you will get value from this book if you are a college or university student preparing for exams, projects, or your first job. You will benefit if you are a fresh graduate joining the IT industry. You will benefit if you are a working professional in software development, IT operations, cybersecurity, networking, cloud, data, customer support, sales, marketing, finance, human resources, legal, healthcare administration, education, or any role that involves reading, writing, analysing, or deciding.

You will benefit if you are a manager or team lead who wants your team to adopt AI tools responsibly. You will benefit if you are a senior leader who wants a clear-eyed view of where these tools shine and where they fail. You will benefit if you are an entrepreneur, freelancer, or consultant looking for an honest competitive edge. The promises and the pitfalls are the same across all these groups; only the examples change.

How to Read This Book

You can read this book front to back, but you do not have to. The first three chapters lay the foundation: what these tools actually are, how to choose between them, and how to write a good prompt. After that, the chapters are organized by use case. Skip to whichever chapter matches the problem on your desk today. Try the prompts. Come back later for the next one. Treat it as a recipe book rather than a novel.

One small request: type the prompts yourself the first time. Resist the urge to just copy and paste. The act of typing slows you down enough to notice the structure of a good prompt, and that noticing is what eventually lets you write your own.

How To Use This Book Effectively

Every chapter in this book follows the same simple structure so that you always know what to expect. Each chapter begins with a short scenario drawn from a realistic working situation. After the scenario, the chapter explains the underlying idea in plain English. Then it gives you one or more ready-to-use prompts. Each prompt is followed by guidance on what a good answer looks like, what to watch out for, and how to refine your follow-up. Finally, every chapter ends with a small set of practice tasks so you can apply what you learned to your own work.

To get the most out of this book, treat each chapter like a one-hour workshop. Read the scenario. Read the explanation. Open the AI tool of your choice on your laptop or phone. Type the prompt yourself; do not just copy and paste. Read the response carefully and ask the AI to refine, expand, or correct things. Then attempt the practice exercise on a real piece of work from your own life: a study topic, a ticket, a draft email, a meeting summary, a report. Practicing on your own work is the single highest-leverage move you can make while reading this book.

Wherever you see a prompt printed in a shaded box, you can copy it word for word, but you will get even better results if you replace the bracketed placeholders with details from your own situation. Wherever you see a tip, take it seriously: the tips capture lessons that took many hours of real-world use to learn. Wherever you see a warning, do not ignore it: the warnings address real failure modes, including hallucinations, privacy mistakes, and ethical traps.

If something does not work for you the first time, the answer is almost never that the AI is broken. Far more often, the prompt was vague, the wrong tool was chosen for the task, or the context the AI needed was missing. This book gives you the patterns to fix all three.

PART I

FOUNDATIONS

What AI assistants are, how they differ, and how to talk to them so they actually help?

Chapter 1

The New Workforce — You and Your AI Co-Worker

A Tuesday Morning in 2026

It is 9:14 in the morning. Priya, a systems administrator at a mid-sized financial services company, opens her laptop. Her inbox has forty-three unread messages. The night-shift handover document is three pages long. Her ticket queue has twenty-eight items, four of them tagged urgent. A vendor has emailed asking for a security questionnaire response by end of day. Her manager has scheduled a one-hour meeting at eleven to plan the next quarter.

Two years ago, Priya would have spent the first ninety minutes of her day just triaging this pile. Today, by 9:32, she has a one-paragraph summary of the handover, a draft prioritized list of tickets that flags the four urgent ones with likely root causes pulled from past similar incidents, a first-pass draft of the vendor security response, and an outline of talking points for the planning meeting. She did not write any of these from scratch. She did not magically become a faster typist. She has simply made an AI assistant a regular collaborator in her morning routine.

This book is about how to do what Priya does, every day, in your own role. It does not require you to be a programmer. It does not require you to be a prompt engineer. It requires you to understand a few clear ideas, learn a small set of habits, and practise on real work. That is all.

What Is an AI Assistant, Really?

Strip away the marketing language and an AI assistant, in the form most working professionals will use it today, is a piece of software that has read an extraordinary amount of human-written text, code, and other digital content. By doing so, it has built a statistical sense of which words and ideas tend to follow which other words and ideas in different contexts. When you give it an instruction, it generates a response by predicting, one piece at a time, what a sensible answer to that instruction would look like.

It is, in other words, a very fluent pattern-matcher. This is its great strength and its main weakness. Because it has read so much, it can write a passable resignation letter, draft a reasonable Python function, summarize a research paper, or explain a network protocol. Because it works by prediction rather than understanding in the way humans understand, it can also confidently produce things that sound right but are wrong. Professionals call this hallucination. The whole craft of using AI well is about getting the strengths and managing the weaknesses.

Three Mental Models That Will Save You

To use AI assistants well in your daily work, three mental models are more useful than any number of feature lists. They are simple, but they will quietly shape every prompt you write.

Model One: The Brilliant Intern

Treat your AI assistant like a brilliant intern on their very first week at your company. The intern is fast, well-read, hardworking, and eager to please. The intern can write competently on almost any topic, can pick up a new tool in an afternoon, and never seems tired. But the intern does not know your colleagues, does not know your customers, has not read your internal documents, has not seen last quarter's results, and will sometimes confidently say things that are subtly or completely wrong because they are trying too hard to be helpful. You would never let this intern send an important email without a quick review. You would not let them push code straight to production. You would, however, gladly let them prepare a first draft, do background research, or break a hard problem into smaller steps.

That is exactly the right way to think about ChatGPT, Gemini, Claude, Grok, and NotebookLM in your work. They are first-draft engines. They make your second draft easier. They will not replace your judgement, your relationships, or your accountability.

Model Two: The Conversation, Not the Command

New users tend to type a single sentence, look at the result, decide it was disappointing, and walk away. Skilled users have a conversation. They start with an instruction, read the answer, then push back, refine, ask follow-up questions, share more context, ask for alternatives, ask the assistant to critique its own answer, and only stop when the result is genuinely useful. This iterative back and forth is where almost all the value lives.

If you remember nothing else from this book, remember this: the best prompt is the second prompt. The second prompt is the one where you tell the assistant what was missing or wrong about its first answer. Get into the habit of always sending at least one follow-up.

Model Three: Garbage In, Gold Out — But Only Sometimes

AI assistants behave like very polite mirrors. If your prompt is vague, the answer will be vague. If your prompt is specific, with role, audience, format, length, tone, and constraints made explicit, the answer will be specific. You will spend a few extra seconds writing the prompt and save many minutes editing the response. This is the single highest-leverage habit in this entire book, and Chapter 3 is devoted to it.

What Has Changed at Work Because of AI

It is worth pausing to acknowledge what has actually changed in the typical workplace over the last few years. Three shifts matter for almost every reader of this book.

The first shift is that the cost of producing a competent first draft of almost anything has fallen close to zero. Whether the draft is an email, a project plan, a SQL query, an incident report, a security policy, a study summary, or a marketing tagline, you can have a credible starting point in under a minute. This means that the rare and valuable skill is no longer producing a draft. The rare and valuable skill is judging a draft, improving it, and integrating it with everything else going on in your work.

The second shift is that knowledge gaps are easier to close than ever. If a colleague mentions a concept, you do not understand, an AI assistant can give you a clear, level-appropriate explanation in seconds. If you encounter a tool, you have never used, you can ask the assistant to explain it as if you were a beginner. This does not replace formal learning, but it shrinks the friction of curiosity. The professionals pulling ahead are the ones who use this to learn more, not less.

The third shift is that the value of clear thinking has gone up, not down. AI assistants amplify whatever direction you point them in. If you point them at a confused question, you will get confused output, faster. If you point them at a clear question, you will get clear output, faster. People who can break a fuzzy problem into a clear set of sub-questions are now dramatically more productive than those who cannot. This book will help you build that habit.

The Five Assistants You Will Meet

This book focuses on five assistants in particular. Each one has strengths, costs, and quirks, and Chapter 2 will give you a side-by-side comparison. Briefly, ChatGPT from OpenAI is the most widely known and a strong all-rounder; Gemini from Google is tightly integrated with Google Workspace and is excellent for tasks that involve search and Google documents; Claude from Anthropic is widely admired for thoughtful long-form writing, careful reasoning, and document analysis; Grok from xAI emphasises real-time information from social posts and a more direct conversational style; and NotebookLM from Google is a specialized tool that lets you upload your own documents and ask grounded questions only about that material.

You do not need all five to begin. Pick one, get fluent, then add others as your needs grow. Throughout this book, when a particular tool is especially well-suited to a task, it will be called out by name.

Practice Exercises

First, sign up for at least one of the five assistants if you have not already. The free tiers are sufficient for almost every example in this book. Spend ten minutes asking it three real questions from your current work or studies. Pay attention to the moment you feel like giving up; that is exactly the moment a follow-up prompt is needed.

Second, write down on paper or in a note three tasks from your last working week that took longer than you wished they had. These will be your private practice list as you work through this book. By the time you reach Chapter 18, you should be able to do all three of them in a fraction of the time.

Third, share with one trusted colleague that you are reading this book. Having a learning partner roughly doubles the chance that the habits will stick. You will also have someone to compare prompts with, which is itself one of the fastest ways to improve.

Chapter 2

Meet the Five Assistants

Why a Tour Matters

Most people pick the first AI assistant they hear about and stick with it. That is a reasonable starting point, but it leaves real value on the table. Each of the five assistants in this book has a personality, a set of strengths, and a few situations where it is clearly the best choice. A short tour of all five will let you choose the right one for the right job, the way a good carpenter chooses between a hammer and a mallet.

ChatGPT (OpenAI)

ChatGPT was the assistant that made AI mainstream. It is a strong all-rounder: it writes well, codes competently, summarises clearly, and reasons through multi-step problems. It has a large ecosystem of features, including custom assistants, image generation, voice mode, and integrations with many third-party tools. For most everyday office work, it is a safe default choice.

Where it shines: drafting emails and reports, brainstorming, learning new topics through conversation, writing and explaining code, generating images, and performing structured analysis when given clear instructions. The free tier is usable; paid tiers unlock more powerful models, longer context, and additional features. Always check the official site for current pricing and feature availability, since these change regularly.

> **NOTE**
>
> Reference: openai.com and chat.openai.com. For the most current information on ChatGPT plans, models, and feature availability, consult the official OpenAI website. Pricing and model names change frequently.

Google Gemini

Gemini is Google's flagship AI assistant. Its biggest practical advantage is integration. If your work lives in Gmail, Google Docs, Google Sheets, Google Slides, Google Drive, or Google Calendar, Gemini can read those documents, draft replies in context, summarize threads, and help build presentations directly within those tools. It also handles very long documents well and has strong multilingual support.

Where it shines: anything where the source material is already in Google's ecosystem; quickly summarizing long PDFs or reports; multilingual drafting; tasks that benefit from up-to-date web knowledge through Google Search.

> **NOTE**
>
> Reference: gemini.google.com. For Google Workspace integrations, see workspace.google.com. Availability and pricing depend on your Google account type and region.

Anthropic Claude

Claude is widely respected for thoughtful, nuanced writing and careful reasoning, particularly on longer documents. It tends to be more conservative when it is unsure, which makes it a favorite among writers, researchers, lawyers, and analysts who value accuracy over flair. It is also strong on code, especially for understanding and refactoring existing code rather than just writing new code from scratch.

Where it shines: long-form writing; analyzing or summarizing long documents and contracts; code review and debugging; structured ethical reasoning; situations where you want the assistant to admit when it does not know rather than guess. Claude is the assistant powering this very book's drafting environment in many use cases.

> **NOTE**
>
> Reference: claude.ai and anthropic.com. Anthropic publishes its usage and safety policies openly; review them before using Claude with any organizational data.

xAI Grok

Grok, from xAI, has a more conversational and direct personality than the other assistants. It is integrated with the X platform (formerly Twitter), which gives it strong real-time awareness of what is being discussed publicly online. For tasks that need a current pulse on news, public sentiment, or very recent events, Grok can be useful as a complement to the other tools.

Where it shines: quick takes on current events; real-time social media awareness; situations where you want a less corporate tone in the response. Like all assistants, its real-time data should still be verified before use in any high-stakes context.

> **NOTE**
>
> Reference: grok.x.ai and x.ai. Access typically requires an X Premium subscription; check the official xAI website for current details.

Google NotebookLM

NotebookLM is the most specialized of the five and the most underused. It is not a general chat assistant. Instead, it lets you upload your own documents — PDFs, Google Docs, web pages, slides, even audio — and then ask grounded questions, get summaries, generate study guides, and create audio briefings based only on the material you have provided. Because it is grounded in your sources, it is much less prone to hallucination than a general chat assistant.

Where it shines: studying for exams from a stack of lecture notes; preparing briefings from internal company documents; analyzing a set of research papers; turning long meeting recordings or compliance documents into readable summaries; preparing for interviews by uploading job descriptions and your resume. Many readers of this book will get more value from NotebookLM than from any other tool, simply because it works on their own real material.

> **NOTE**
>
> Reference: notebooklm.google.com. Always check the privacy and data-handling terms before uploading sensitive material, and never upload classified, regulated, or client-confidential data without explicit organizational approval.

A Quick Decision Guide

Use ChatGPT or Claude as your everyday all-rounder. Use Gemini when your source material lives in Google Workspace or when you need fresh web information. Use Claude when the task involves careful reading, long-form writing, or nuanced analysis. Use Grok when you specifically need a feel for live discussion on the X platform. Use NotebookLM whenever the task is grounded in a specific set of documents you can upload. Most readers settle on a primary, a secondary, and NotebookLM for document work, and that combination is more than enough for ninety percent of professional needs.

How to Choose, Practically

If you are starting from zero and want a single recommendation: begin with ChatGPT or Claude on the free tier, and add NotebookLM the moment you have a stack of documents you actually need to read. You can comfortably do the rest of this book with that combination. Add the others as curiosity and need dictate.

> **TIP**
>
> Bookmark all five assistant home pages in a single browser folder named 'AI Tools.' Open them in separate tabs at the start of any complex task. The friction of switching becomes invisible once they are all one click away.

Chapter 3

The Art of the Prompt

The Most Important Chapter in This Book

If you read only one chapter of this book carefully, make it this one. Everything else builds on the small set of habits introduced here. The good news is that the habits are simple. The better news is that they take effect immediately. The moment you start writing prompts using the patterns in this chapter, the quality of every response you receive will visibly improve.

The CRISP Framework

Many prompt frameworks exist, but most are over-engineered. The simplest one that consistently produces strong results in everyday office work is what this book will call CRISP: Context, Role, Instruction, Specifics, and Polish. Whenever you sit down to write a prompt for any non-trivial task, mentally run through these five letters. Each letter answers a single question.

Context: What background information does the assistant need in order to give a good answer? Who is the audience? What is the situation? Role: What hat should the assistant wear? An expert in what? A teacher of what? A colleague at what level of seniority? Instruction: What, exactly, do you want the assistant to produce? A draft? A summary? A list? A critique? Specifics: What format, length, tone, and constraints apply? Are there things to include or avoid? Polish: A short instruction at the end inviting the assistant to ask clarifying questions before answering, or to flag uncertainty if any.

Most disappointing prompts skip three or four of the five elements. Most excellent prompts include all five. That is the entire secret.

From Weak to Strong: A Worked Example

Suppose you need to write a follow-up email to a vendor whose product demo went poorly. A weak prompt looks like this:

> **Weak Prompt**
> `Write an email to the vendor about the demo.`

This will produce a generic, slightly stiff email. Now compare a CRISP-shaped version of the same task:

> 🎯 **Strong Prompt (CRISP)**
>
> ```
> Context: I am the IT manager at a mid-sized retail company. Yesterday, a vendor demoed their endpoint security product to my team. The demo was disorganized, several features did not work, and the presenter could not answer basic questions about pricing. Role: Act as a polite but firm IT procurement manager who values vendor relationships but also values our team's time. Instruction: Draft a professional email to our vendor account manager, Sara, summarizing what went wrong, requesting a redo with a more prepared technical lead, and asking for written answers to three specific questions: pricing for 500 endpoints, support SLAs, and whether the product integrates with our SIEM. Specifics: Length about 200 words, tone polite and professional but clearly disappointed, no exclamation marks, and end with a clear next step. Polish: If anything is unclear, ask before drafting. Once you draft it, also suggest one shorter alternative version I could use as a Slack message instead.
> ```

Notice how much more is now possible. The assistant knows your industry, your role, the situation, the relationship dynamics, the format, the length, the tone, and the next steps. The first draft will be ninety percent of the way to a final email.

Five Habits That Multiply Results

Habit One: Always Set the Role

Telling the assistant who to be transforms its tone. 'Act as a senior cybersecurity consultant explaining this to a board of non-technical directors' produces a very different answer than 'Act as a security engineer writing a peer technical brief,' even if the underlying topic is the same. Get into the habit of starting non-trivial prompts with a role.

Habit Two: Specify the Audience

Almost everything you produce at work is written for a specific audience: a customer, a manager, a regulator, an end user, a peer team. State the audience explicitly. 'Explain this to a final-year computer science student' yields a very different result from 'Explain this to a non-technical executive sponsor.' The assistant cannot guess; it can only respond to what you give it.

Habit Three: Constrain the Format

Tell the assistant exactly what shape the output should take: a numbered list, a table with three columns, a 200-word paragraph, a short email with a subject line, a script of dialogue, a checklist. Free-form output is harder to use; structured output is ready to drop into your work.

Habit Four: Iterate Without Apology

Treat the first response as a starting point, not a verdict. Ask the assistant to make it shorter. Make it more formal. Make it more critical. Add a counter-argument. Rewrite it for an Indian audience. Translate it into Tamil. Add a bullet list of risks. Each follow-up sharpens the result.

Habit Five: Make It Self-Critique

After a long answer, type: 'Now critique your previous answer as if you were a skeptical senior reviewer. List five weaknesses or risks in it. Then revise.' This single habit catches more mistakes than almost any other technique. The assistant is often more honest about flaws when explicitly invited to find them.

Common Pitfalls to Avoid

There are a small number of mistakes that account for most of the bad experiences people have with AI assistants. Watch for them in your own usage.

The first pitfall is being vague and then blaming the tool. If you ask 'help me with my project' you will get a vague answer. If you give the assistant the project's goal, current state, audience, deadline, and the specific bottleneck you are stuck on, you will get specific help. The assistant is not psychic; it works with what you give it.

The second pitfall is trusting the first answer without verification. AI assistants can produce confident-sounding nonsense, especially with numbers, dates, citations, regulations, and very recent events. Always verify anything that will be used in a decision, a publication, or a customer-facing artefact. Treat the assistant as a draftsman, not a source of truth.

The third pitfall is pasting in confidential information without thinking. Before pasting customer data, source code from internal systems, contracts, financials, or personally identifiable information into any AI assistant, check your organization's policy and the tool's data-handling terms. Chapter 16 covers this in depth.

> ⚠ **WARNING**
>
> Never paste passwords, API keys, customer personal data, regulated health or financial records, or proprietary source code into a public AI assistant without explicit organizational approval and a clear understanding of how that data will be retained, used for training, and protected. When in doubt, redact, summarize, or use an enterprise tier with appropriate data-handling guarantees.

Building Your Own Prompt Library

By the end of this book, you will have written hundreds of prompts. The best ones are too valuable to retype every time. Open a simple notes file or document and start saving the prompts that worked particularly well. Tag them by use case: email, status report, code review, log analysis, meeting summary, learning. Within a few weeks you will have a personal prompt library worth more than any book, because it is shaped to your work. Appendix A at the end of this book gives you a starter library of forty prompts to seed your own.

Practice Exercises

To lock in the lessons of this chapter, complete the following before moving on to Part II. First, take any task you completed in the last week and write a CRISP-shaped prompt for it. Run it through your chosen assistant. Compare the result to what you actually produced. Second, take a one-line vague prompt you have used in the past and rewrite it using all five CRISP elements; observe how the response changes. Third, run the self-critique habit on a real piece of writing, such as a draft email, by pasting it in and asking the assistant to critique it as a skeptical senior reviewer. Notice which feedback you would never have given yourself.

PART II

AI FOR EVERYDAY OFFICE WORK

Email, meetings, writing, and presentations: the ninety percent of work that fills most calendars.

Chapter 4

Email, Reports, and Documentation

Scenario: The Friday Afternoon Inbox

It is four o'clock on Friday afternoon. Ramesh, a project manager, is staring at his inbox. He has nineteen emails that need substantive replies, a weekly status report due to the steering committee in an hour, and a customer escalation that needs a careful written response. Two years ago, he would have skipped lunch on Monday to catch up. Today, he opens his AI assistant and works through the pile in forty minutes. The status report is one well-shaped prompt. The customer reply is two prompts. The other emails are a mix of templates, summaries, and short drafts. By five fifteen he is closing his laptop.

This chapter is about how Ramesh works. The techniques are simple, repeatable, and apply equally to a graduate trainee answering their first internal email and a senior leader writing a quarterly board update.

Drafting Emails That Match the Moment

Most professional emails fall into a small number of categories: a request, a status update, a follow-up, a polite refusal, a difficult message, an introduction, or a thank you. Once you can prompt confidently for each category, you can write any email in your working life faster and better.

The Universal Email Prompt

> **Universal Email Drafter**
>
> `Act as a [your role and seniority] writing to [audience: peer / customer / vendor / manager / team / regulator]. The goal of the email is to [single clear objective]. Key points to include: - [point 1] - [point 2] - [point 3] Tone: [warm and informal / neutral and professional / firm and formal / apologetic and constructive]. Length: about [number] words. End with a clear next step. If you need any context to write this well, ask me first. After drafting, suggest one shorter alternative I could send as a quick chat message.`

Notice the structure: who you are, who you are writing to, the goal, the points, the tone, the length, the next step, and an invitation to clarify. Almost every prompt in this chapter will follow that same skeleton.

The Difficult Message

AI assistants are unusually good at the kind of email most professionals dread writing: a polite refusal, a delayed delivery, a missed deadline, or a corrective note. They take the emotional charge out of the first draft, leaving you to add the human touch in the second.

> **Delayed Delivery Email**
>
> `Act as a delivery manager writing to a customer who is expecting a deliverable that will be one week late. The customer is generally reasonable but has been frustrated by previous delays. Draft a brief, professional email that owns the delay without making excuses, explains the cause in one short sentence, presents a credible new date, offers one small gesture of goodwill, and closes with confidence. About 150 words, no apologies more than once, no jargon.`

Writing Reports That People Actually Read

The single biggest mistake in workplace reports is burying the conclusion. Readers, especially senior ones, want to know the answer first and the reasoning second. A well-prompted AI assistant can restructure even a rambling first draft into a tight, top-down report in minutes.

The Status Report Prompt

> **Weekly Status Report**
>
> Act as my chief of staff. Below are my notes from this week. Turn them into a one-page weekly status report for my manager. Structure:
>
> 1. Headline: one sentence summarizing the week.
> 2. Wins: three bullet points.
> 3. Risks and blockers: each with a one-line owner and next step.
> 4. Asks: anything I need from my manager.
> 5. Next week: three priorities. Keep it factual, no marketing language, total length about 250 words. My notes: [paste your raw notes here]

This single prompt, used consistently every Friday, will save the average manager between thirty and ninety minutes per week. Many readers will find the structural discipline alone is more valuable than the time saved.

The Long Report Compression Prompt

When you receive a long document and need to brief someone in a hurry, the following prompt is your best friend. NotebookLM is especially powerful for this kind of work because it grounds the summary in the source document.

> **Document Compression for Executives**
>
> Below is a [type of document, e.g. vendor whitepaper, internal report, research paper, regulation]. Produce three layered summaries:
>
> 1. Thirty-second elevator version (about 50 words).
> 2. Two-minute briefing (about 200 words, with the three most important takeaways and any decision required).
> 3. One-page deeper summary (about 500 words, structured into background, key findings, implications, and open questions). Flag any claim in the document that I should personally verify before relying on it. Document: [paste or attach]

Documentation: The Hidden Work That Pays Forever

Almost every IT and corporate role has an under-served documentation backlog. Runbooks that have not been updated in two years. Onboarding guides written for a system that no longer exists. Knowledge articles that nobody can find. AI assistants are extraordinarily good at this kind of work because the raw material usually exists somewhere, just not in a usable shape. Your job is to gather it; the assistant's job is to structure it.

The Runbook Prompt

Operational Runbook Generator

```
Act as a senior site reliability engineer. I am going to describe a recurring incident scenario and the steps my team currently takes to resolve it. Turn that into a clean operational runbook with the following sections: - Title and one-line description - When this runbook applies (symptoms, alerts, triggering conditions) - Pre-checks before starting - Step-by-step resolution, numbered, with the exact commands or console paths to use - Verification steps - Rollback plan - Post-incident actions and where to log them - Escalation path with role names, not personal names Write in clear British English, third person, present tense. If any step is ambiguous, mark it with a TODO and a clarifying question I should answer. Scenario and current steps: [your description]
```

TIP

Once you have a runbook draft, paste it back into the assistant and ask: 'Now critique this runbook from the perspective of a tired engineer at 2 a.m. who has never read it before. Where would they get stuck?' This single follow-up exposes ambiguity that no first draft catches.

Templates That Compound Over Time

The truly senior move is to stop writing one-off prompts and start building reusable templates. Save your best prompts in a personal document. Tag them. Refine them as you learn. Within three months you will have a private toolkit that your colleagues do not even know exists, and your output will start to look magical to them. It is not magic. It is the same kind of leverage that spreadsheets gave the previous generation, made personal.

Practice Exercises

First, take the next email you would normally have to write and run it through the universal email drafter prompt above. Note how much editing the result needs. Second, take last week's status update and feed your raw notes through the status report prompt; compare the structure to what you originally wrote. Third, identify one undocumented process on your team and use the runbook prompt to produce a first draft, then send it to a colleague for review.

Chapter 5

Meetings, Minutes, and the End of the Notes Backlog

Scenario: Six Meetings, Zero Notes

Anjali, a product manager, has back-to-back meetings from nine to four every Tuesday. By the end of the day, she has scribbled handwritten notes that nobody else will ever read, and a vague memory of who agreed to what. Her team waits two days for action items. By Thursday, half the action items have shifted in her memory, and she has to ask people to re-confirm what they had committed to.

AI tools have quietly solved this problem for any team willing to adopt a few new habits. Recordings or transcripts go in; a clean summary, action items by owner, and a draft follow-up email come out. Done well, this single workflow gives back two to four hours every week.

Three Levels of Meeting Support

How much AI helps with meetings depends on what your meeting platform allows and what your organization permits. Three levels are common in 2026, and the prompts in this chapter work for all three.

The first level is post-meeting: you transcribe or record, then paste the transcript into an assistant. The second level is in-meeting tools that produce live transcripts, summaries, and action items, often built into the meeting platform itself. The third level is purpose-built notetaking assistants that join the meeting as a participant.

> ⚠ **WARNING**
>
> Recording or transcribing a meeting may be legally regulated in your country and against your organization's policy. Always inform participants, get consent, and follow your data protection rules. Do not record meetings involving regulated personal data, sensitive HR matters, or legal privilege without explicit guidance from your legal or compliance team.

The Meeting Distillation Prompt

> **Meeting Notes Distiller**
>
> Below is the transcript of a [duration]-minute meeting between [number] participants on the topic of [topic]. Produce the following, in this order:
>
> 1. One-sentence headline of the meeting outcome.
> 2. Decisions made (bullet points, each with the rationale in one short clause).
> 3. Action items (table format with columns: Owner, Action, Due date, Status). If the owner or due date was not stated, mark TBD and flag it at the end.
> 4. Open questions or items deferred to next meeting.
> 5. A short follow-up email I can send to attendees (about 120 words), thanking them, summarizing decisions, and listing actions. Use neutral, factual language. Do not invent any decision, action, or date that was not in the transcript. If something was discussed inconclusively, say so. Transcript: [paste]

Preparing for Meetings, Not Just Documenting Them

Documentation is only half the value. The other half is preparation. Walking into a meeting with a clear agenda, a set of well-shaped questions, and an awareness of likely objections will make you visibly more effective than colleagues who walk in cold.

> **Meeting Preparation Brief**
>
> I have a one-hour meeting tomorrow with [audience and their role/seniority]. The objective is to [single clear objective]. The context is [brief background]. Produce:
>
> 1. A proposed agenda with time boxes that totals 55 minutes (leaving 5 minutes for buffer).
> 2. The five most important questions I should ask, ordered by priority.
> 3. The three most likely objections or pushback I will receive, with a one-line response strategy for each.
> 4. One unconventional question that might surface a hidden assumption.
> 5. A short pre-read I can send to attendees the night before (about 100 words). Keep it pragmatic, not formal.

Decision Memos and One-Pagers

Some of the highest-leverage writing in any organization is the humble decision memo: a one-page document that frames a decision, the options, and a recommendation. AI assistants make these dramatically easier to produce, especially in their classic structure: context, options, recommendation, risks, asks.

> ⚖ **Decision Memo Generator**
>
> ```
> Act as a senior consultant. Below are my rough notes on a decision my team needs to make. Turn them into a one-page decision memo with the following structure: - Title (one line, action-oriented) - Context (3-4 sentences) - Options considered (a table with columns: Option, Pros, Cons, estimated effort, estimated risk) - Recommendation (clear, with reasoning in 3 sentences) - Key risks and mitigations - Decision required from whom by when Formal but plain English. No filler. About 400 words. My notes: [paste]
> ```

Practice Exercises

First, run your most recent meeting through the distillation prompt. Compare what the AI captured to your own memory; you will be surprised how much you forgot. Second, prepare for your next important meeting using the meeting preparation brief prompt. Notice whether you walk in feeling more confident. Third, take a decision your team is currently debating and run it through the decision memo prompt; share the result with your manager and watch how the conversation shifts.

Chapter 6

Presentations, Pitches, and Telling a Clear Story

Scenario: The Slide Deck Due Tomorrow

Vikram has been asked to present the Q3 roadmap to senior leadership tomorrow morning. It is now nine in the evening. The roadmap exists in his head and in scattered documents, but no slide deck has been started. Two years ago, this would have been an all-nighter. Today, he opens his AI assistant, sketches out the storyline, generates a slide outline, drafts the speaker notes, and uses Google Gemini's integration with Slides to produce a clean first version. By eleven, he is reviewing the deck with a glass of water rather than panic.

Storytelling Is the Real Skill

A good presentation is a story before it is a slide deck. A clear story has a problem, a tension, a turning point, and a resolution. Most workplace decks fail because they are organized around topics rather than stories. AI assistants are remarkably good at helping you find the story buried in your material, if you ask them to.

📖 **Story-First Deck Outline**

```
Act as a senior communications coach. I need to deliver a [duration]-minute presentation to [audience]. The objective is [outcome I want]. The key facts I have are [list].  First, propose three possible narrative arcs for this presentation, each in 3-4 sentences. Recommend the strongest one and say why. Then, for the recommended arc, produce a slide-by-slide outline with: - Slide title (short, opinionated, not generic) - One-sentence message that the slide must communicate - 3 bullet points of supporting content - A 60-word speaker note Keep total slides between 8 and

12.Avoid corporate clichés.
```

Designing Slides That Do Not Look Like Noise

AI assistants will not, on their own, produce beautifully designed slides. What they can do is enforce structural discipline: one message per slide, supporting points in parallel grammar, headlines that are statements rather than topics, and an overall logical flow. Those structural choices matter more for the audience than any animation or colour scheme.

> **TIP**
>
> Replace every topic-style slide title (such as 'Q3 Performance') with a sentence-style title that states the message ('Q3 Revenue Grew 18%, Driven by Two New Markets'). This single habit transforms how decks are received in senior meetings.

Pitches and Persuasion

If you ever need to pitch an idea, a project, or a product, the assistant can be your invisible coach. Use it to stress-test your pitch by asking it to play the role of a skeptical investor, a busy executive, or a difficult customer.

```
Pitch Stress Test
I am about to pitch [idea/project/product] to [audience]. Below is my draft pitch. First, score it from 1 to 10 on: clarity, credibility, urgency, differentiation, and call to action. Then, role-play as a skeptical senior decision-maker and ask the five hardest questions you would ask after hearing this pitch. For each question, briefly explain why it would be hard. Finally, suggest three concrete edits that would raise the lowest two scores by at least two points each. My pitch: [paste]
```

Audience Adaptation

The same idea must be told differently to a board, a technical team, a customer, and a regulator. Rather than write four versions yourself, write one master version and ask the assistant to adapt it. Be explicit about what changes between versions: vocabulary, level of detail, examples, and the question the audience cares most about.

Audience Adaptation Prompt

```
Below is a draft executive summary. Produce three adapted versions:
1. For our engineering team (more technical detail, specific tools
   and metrics).
2. For our customers (benefit-led language, no internal jargon,
   includes a clear next step).
3. For our board of directors (financial framing, risk and return,
   three clear strategic implications). Keep each adaptation between
   200 and 250 words. Note in one sentence at the end of each what
   you changed and why. Draft: [paste]
```

Practice Exercises

First, take any presentation you delivered in the last six months and run its content through the story-first deck outline prompt; observe how the new structure compares to what you actually presented. Second, take a current pitch or proposal and run it through the pitch stress test; address at least two of the five hardest questions in your next revision. Third, take any internal document and run it through the audience adaptation prompt for two different audiences relevant to your role.

PART III

AI FOR THE IT PROFESSIONAL

Code, operations, troubleshooting, cloud, and DevOps: making the technical work faster and clearer.

Chapter 7

AI for Software Development and Code Review

Scenario: The Bug at 5:45 p.m.

Karthik, a backend developer, finds a critical bug in production at 5:45 p.m. on a Thursday. The stack trace points to a payment service. He has never worked on that service before. The original author left the company six months ago. Two years ago, this would have been a long evening with a wiki, a coffee, and a lot of guesswork. Today, he opens the codebase, pastes the relevant function and the stack trace into Claude or ChatGPT, and within a few exchanges has a clear hypothesis, a candidate fix, a regression test, and a draft message to the on-call channel.

This chapter is about how that conversation goes, and how you can have it on demand for the code in your own world.

How AI Helps the Whole Software Lifecycle

AI assistants can help across every stage of writing software, but their value differs at each stage. They are extremely good at explanation, refactoring, generating tests, debugging, code review, and producing boilerplate. They are moderately good at writing entirely new code from scratch, especially in well-known domains. They are poor at reading your private business rules, your team's coding standards, and the political subtext of why a particular module exists. The best engineers use AI for the first list and use their own judgement for the second.

Explaining Unfamiliar Code

The fastest way to onboard yourself to a codebase you have never seen is to ask the assistant to explain it. Crucially, ask for an explanation that you can follow, given your background. Tell it what you already know.

```
</> Code Explainer

Below is a function from a codebase I am new to. Explain it in plain English, assuming I am a [your level, e.g. mid-level Python developer] who is comfortable with [language and frameworks you know] but unfamiliar with [unfamiliar tech]. For your explanation:
1. State the purpose of the function in one sentence.
2. Walk through it block by block.
3. Identify any non-obvious behavior, edge cases, or hidden assumptions.
4. Suggest two questions I should ask the team about this code.
5. Identify any code smells or risks. Code: [paste]
```

Debugging With an AI Pair

Debugging is where AI assistants earn their place on every developer's screen. The trick is to give the assistant everything it needs in a single prompt: the symptom, the relevant code, the stack trace if any, what you have already tried, and what you suspect.

```
Debug Companion

I am debugging an issue in [language and framework]. Here is what I am observing: Symptom: [describe what is wrong] Expected behavior: [what should happen] What I have already tried: [list] My current hypothesis: [if any] Relevant code: [paste minimal reproducible example] Stack trace / logs: [paste] Produce:
1. A ranked list of the three most likely root causes, each with a short reason.
2. For the most likely cause, an exact code-level fix.
3. A regression test (in [test framework]) that would have caught this bug.
4. One question you would ask if you needed more information.
```

Writing Tests, You Will Not Skip

Most developers know they should write more tests. Most do not. AI assistants change the cost-benefit equation: a credible test suite for a function can be generated in a single prompt and refined in two. Treat this as a chance to push test coverage up, not down, on your team.

> **⚡ Test Generator**
>
> Below are a function and its description. Generate a thorough test suite in [test framework, e.g. pytest, JUnit, Jest]. Function: [paste] Description of intended behavior: [paste] Produce tests covering: - Happy path with typical inputs - All identifiable edge cases (empty inputs, null/None, boundary values, very large or very small values) - Invalid input types - Concurrency or order-dependence if relevant - One property-based or fuzz-style test if appropriate For each test, add a one-line comment explaining what behavior it is verifying. Use clear, behavioral test names (e.g. test_returns_zero_when_input_list_is_empty).

Code Review as a Sparring Partner

Before submitting a pull request, run your own code through the assistant as a skeptical senior reviewer. The feedback is rarely mind-blowing, but it catches the small mistakes that human reviewers find tedious to flag, freeing them to focus on architecture and intent.

> **🔍 Pre-PR Code Review**
>
> Act as a skeptical senior engineer reviewing a pull request. Below is a diff (or full file). Review it for:
>
> 1. Correctness and edge cases
> 2. Readability and naming
> 3. Performance concerns
> 4. Security issues (especially injection, authentication, authorization, secrets)
> 5. Test coverage adequacy
> 6. Adherence to common best practices in [language] For each issue, give: severity (low/medium/high), exact file/line if possible, the concern, and a concrete suggested change. End with three positive observations about the code. Code: [paste]

Refactoring Without Fear

Refactoring legacy code is one of the most rewarding uses of AI assistance. Paste in a tangled function, describe the contract you need to preserve, and ask for a cleaner version with explanations of what changed and why.

> ⚠ **WARNING**
>
> Always run the existing test suite against the AI's refactored output before trusting it. If no test suite exists, generate one against the original behavior first, then refactor against the tests. Never replace working production code with AI output that has not been tested.

Practice Exercises

First, take any function from your current codebase and run it through the code explainer prompt; you will likely learn something even about code you wrote yourself. Second, the next time you hit a bug, force yourself to use the debug companion prompt before any console.log debugging; compare which approach was faster. Third, generate a test suite for an untested utility function in your code; commit it. Many readers find that this single chapter changes how they work for years.

Chapter 8

AI for IT Operations and Support

Scenario: Two A.M. Alert Storm

Sneha is on call. At 2:14 a.m., her pager fires off five alerts in seven minutes. Her sleep-deprived brain has to triage them, find the common cause if any, and decide which to wake teammates for. She opens her laptop, pastes the alerts and the recent change log into her assistant, and asks it to correlate, hypothesize, and rank. Within three minutes she has a working theory, a suggested first action, and a draft incident channel message. She is not skipping her judgement; she is sharpening it with a faster first pass.

Triage and Correlation

> 🚨 **Alert Triage Helper**
>
> I am the on-call engineer for a [type of system, e.g. e-commerce backend running on AWS with Kubernetes]. In the last 10 minutes the following alerts fired (in time order): [paste alerts with timestamps] The most recent deploys/changes in the last 24 hours were: [paste] Produce:
>
> 1. The two or three most likely root-cause hypotheses, ranked.
> 2. For each, the next two diagnostic commands or queries I should run, with exact syntax.
> 3. The single safest first action I can take to reduce customer impact while I confirm.
> 4. A draft incident channel post (about 80 words) summarizing what we know and the next update time.
> 5. A short list of questions for the team if we need to escalate.

Writing Help-Desk Replies That Help

Whether you work an internal IT helpdesk or external customer support, AI assistants can transform the quality of your written replies. The pattern: paste the user's ticket, describe what you have learned, and ask the assistant to draft a clear, polite, structured reply that fits your organization's voice.

> 💬 **Helpdesk Reply Drafter**
>
> `I am responding to an internal helpdesk ticket. Below is the user's message and the technical answer I want to convey. Draft a reply that: - Acknowledges the user's frustration in one sentence (without being insincere) - States what was done, in plain non-technical language - Provides the answer or workaround clearly, in numbered steps if applicable - Sets expectations for any pending work, with realistic timelines - Closes with a direct invitation to reply if the issue is not resolved Tone: friendly but professional. Length about 120 words. Avoid technical jargon unless the user used it themselves. User's message: [paste] Technical answer to convey: [paste]`

Building Better Knowledge-Base Articles

Ticket queues are gold mines for knowledge-based content. After you resolve a ticket, take a moment to ask the assistant to turn it into a knowledge article. Over a few months, the resulting library will reduce the same kind of tickets significantly.

> 🖭 **Ticket-to-Knowledge-Article**
>
> `Below is a resolved support ticket. Turn it into a clean knowledge-based article with the following structure: - Title (in question form, as users would search for it) - Symptom / who this affects - Cause (one paragraph in plain language) - Resolution (numbered steps with exact paths or commands where applicable) - Verification - Related articles (suggest 2-3 likely related topics) - Tags / keywords for search Write for a non-technical end user. About 350 words. Ticket: [paste]`

Scripting Boring Tasks Away

AI assistants are particularly good at producing the small operational scripts that fill an IT professional's day: a quick PowerShell script to bulk-rename files, a Bash one-liner to grep through logs, a Python utility to convert between formats. Use them to retire your repetitive tasks.

```
⚡ Quick Operational Script
Write a [PowerShell / Bash / Python] script that does the following:
[describe the task in plain English, including inputs, outputs, error
handling expectations, and any environmental constraints like OS
version] Requirements: - Include argument validation - Print clear
progress messages - Handle the obvious failure modes gracefully (file
not found, permission denied, network errors) - Be idempotent if run
twice in a row - Include a brief comment block at the top explaining
usage After the script, list three things I should test before running
this in production.
```

Practice Exercises

First, take the last incident your team handled and run the alert triage helper prompt as a hindsight exercise; compare its hypothesis ranking with the actual root cause. Second, take a recently resolved ticket and produce a knowledge article from it using the prompt above. Third, identify one repetitive operational task that takes you more than ten minutes per week and use the operational script prompt to retire it.

Chapter 9

AI for Cloud, DevOps, and Automation

Scenario: The Terraform Tangle

Rohit's team has inherited a Terraform repository written by three different people over two years. It works, mostly. But every change is risky, the modules overlap confusingly, and nobody fully understands the network configuration. He spends a Sunday morning pasting modules into Claude, asking for explanations and refactoring suggestions, and ends the morning with a clean architecture diagram, a list of risks, and a phased refactor plan. None of this replaces the team's ownership; all of it makes the team's job easier.

Infrastructure as Code, Read Like Prose

```
☁ IaC Explainer
Below is a [Terraform / CloudFormation / Pulumi / ARM / Bicep]
configuration for a [target environment, e.g. AWS production VPC].
Produce:
1. A plain-English summary of what this code provisions, in three
   short paragraphs.
2. A simple ASCII or text-based diagram of the resources and their
   relationships.
3. A list of every external dependency or assumption (variable values
   expected, IAM permissions needed, prerequisite resources).
4. A risk assessment of the top 5 things that could go wrong on apply.
5. Three suggestions to improve readability or modularity, with a
   brief reasoning for each. Code: [paste]
```

Pipelines That Explain Themselves

CI/CD pipeline definitions are notoriously hard to read once they grow past a hundred lines. Use the assistant to summarize, document, and refactor them.

CI/CD Pipeline Summary

```
Below is a [GitHub Actions / GitLab CI / Jenkins / Azure DevOps]
pipeline. Produce:
1. A high-level summary of what each stage does.
2. A flowchart-style description showing trigger, jobs, dependencies,
   and artifact flow.
3. A list of secrets and environment variables this pipeline reads,
   with a guess at where each likely comes from.
4. A list of the three slowest or most flaky-looking parts and why
   they look that way.
5. A list of three concrete improvements that would shorten the
   feedback loop or improve reliability. Pipeline: [paste]
```

Cloud Cost Sanity Checks

Cloud bills grow quietly. AI assistants can be a useful first-pass cost reviewer when fed a billing summary and a description of the workload.

Cloud Cost Reviewer

```
Below is a [provider, e.g. AWS] cost summary for the last billing
period, broken down by service. The workload is described as [brief
description, e.g. a SaaS analytics product with mostly daytime
traffic, 10 microservices, a single region]. For this profile:
1. Identify any line items that look unusually high relative to the
   workload description.
2. Suggest the three highest-impact cost optimizations to investigate,
   with a one-line reason each.
3. Flag any signs of waste (idle instances, untagged resources, over-
   provisioned databases, cross-AZ traffic, expensive log retention)
   that the data suggests.
4. Recommend three monitoring or governance changes that would prevent
   surprises next month. Keep recommendations grounded; do not invent
   specific numbers that are not in the data. Cost summary: [paste]
```

> ⚠ **WARNING**
>
> Cloud cost data and infrastructure code can reveal a lot about an organization's architecture, customers, and weaknesses. Be careful where you paste it. For sensitive environments, use enterprise-grade AI offerings with appropriate data-handling guarantees, or strip identifiers, account IDs, and resource names before sharing.

Automation, the Last Mile

Many tasks in operations are not technically hard but are tedious enough that they keep slipping. AI assistants are excellent at building the connective tissue: small scripts, scheduled jobs, webhooks, and integration glue. Use them to close the gap between what your team plans to automate and what is actually automated.

Practice Exercises

First, paste a Terraform or CloudFormation module from your team's repository into the IaC explainer prompt and share the resulting summary with a teammate; see how their understanding compares. Second, run your team's current CI pipeline through the pipeline summary prompt and identify one improvement to ship this sprint. Third, pull a recent cloud bill, run it through the cost reviewer prompt, and bring the results to your next finance review.

PART IV

AI FOR CYBERSECURITY

From SOC analyst to CISO: using AI to defend, detect, respond, and document with discipline.

Chapter 10

AI for the Security Analyst's Daily Workflow

Scenario: 200 Alerts Before Lunch

Meera is a tier-one analyst in a security operations center. By lunch on a typical Tuesday, she has triaged just over two hundred alerts. Most are false positives. A handful require deeper investigation. Two might be real incidents. Two years ago, the bottleneck was reading. She had to scan logs, lookup IPs, decode commands, and sift through threat intelligence by hand. Today, she uses AI assistants to do the first-pass reading at speed, while keeping every decision and every escalation in her own hands. The result is not that her job is easier in some woolly sense; it is that her attention now lands on the right alerts faster.

This chapter is about building that skill set. It applies to SOC analysts, blue-team engineers, threat hunters, IT staff who handle security on the side, and anyone else who reads logs for a living. The book takes a defender's stance throughout: every example is oriented toward protecting systems, not attacking them. Where techniques could cut both ways, the framing is conservative.

> ⚠ **WARNING**
>
> This chapter assumes you are a defender with explicit authorization to work on the systems and data you are analyzing. Do not use these techniques against systems you do not own or have written permission to test. Always follow your organization's data handling, privacy, and incident-response policies. If your work involves regulated data, prefer enterprise AI offerings with appropriate contracts and data-handling guarantees.

Reading Logs, Faster but Not Lazier

The fastest way to misuse AI in security work is to paste in a log and accept whatever the assistant says. That is exactly the wrong habit. The correct habit is to use the assistant as a fast first reader that surfaces patterns, hypotheses, and questions, while you remain the final analyst. The prompts in this chapter are written to keep you, not the assistant, in charge.

> 📃 **Log Triage Helper**
>
> Below is a [type of log, e.g. authentication log, web server access log, EDR detection summary] from a [system description]. Produce:
>
> 1. A short factual description of what the log shows, in plain language.
> 2. The three most suspicious patterns or entries, ranked by suspicion. For each, explain why it is suspicious in one or two sentences and reference the specific lines or fields.
> 3. The three most likely benign explanations for each suspicious pattern, so I do not anchor on a malicious interpretation.
> 4. The next two queries or pivots I should run to confirm or deny suspicion (specify exactly what to search for and where).
> 5. A short list of fields or values that are missing from this log but would help me decide. Do not invent log entries that are not present. If something is ambiguous, say so explicitly. Log: [paste, with sensitive identifiers redacted]

Decoding the Obfuscated

Attackers often hide their hand using base64, URL encoding, hex, PowerShell obfuscation, or simple character substitution. Asking an AI assistant to decode and explain these payloads is one of the most reliably useful uses in security work, because the underlying transformations are well-understood and the output can be cross-checked.

> **Suspicious Payload Decoder**
>
> Below is a string I observed in [where, e.g. a PowerShell command line, a URL parameter, an email attachment]. It looks obfuscated.
>
> 1. Identify the encoding(s) used.
> 2. Decode it step by step, showing each intermediate form.
> 3. Once decoded, explain in plain English what the underlying code or text is attempting to do.
> 4. Flag specific behaviors that map to common adversary techniques (e.g., persistence, credential access, defense evasion). Reference MITRE ATT&CK technique IDs only if you are confident; otherwise say uncertain.
> 5. Suggest two defensive actions I should consider immediately. Do not actually execute or fetch any URLs. Treat the input as untrusted.
>   String: [paste]

> **NOTE**
>
> Reference: MITRE ATT&CK is a publicly available knowledge base of adversary tactics and techniques, maintained at attack.mitre.org. Throughout this book, technique IDs are mentioned as a shared vocabulary; verify them against the official site before citing in formal reports.

Indicator Enrichment

When you have an IP address, a domain, a file hash, or a user agent string and need to enrich it, the assistant cannot replace authoritative threat intelligence platforms. It can, however, give you a structured first read that helps you formulate the right queries to the right tools.

> **Indicator First Read**
>
> Below is an indicator I observed in our environment, and the context in which it appeared. Indicator: [IP / domain / hash / user agent] Context: [brief description of how, when, and where it appeared] Produce:
>
> 1. A factual structural read of the indicator (for IP: rough geolocation hint based on common ranges, IPv4/IPv6, public/private; for domain: registrar style, TLD, length and entropy hints suggesting DGA-likeness; for hash: hash type and length).
> 2. A list of the four authoritative sources I should check next (name them and explain what each will tell me).
> 3. The three queries I should run in our SIEM and EDR (give exact field names and patterns I should look for).
> 4. A list of common false-positive scenarios for an indicator like this. Do not assert that this indicator is malicious or benign without external verification. Be explicit that this is a first read, not a verdict.

Writing Detection Logic

Whether you write Sigma rules, Splunk SPL, KQL, Elastic queries, or YARA signatures, AI assistants are useful drafting partners. Always tune and test the output in your own environment before relying on it.

> 🎯 **Detection Rule Drafter**
>
> Act as a senior detection engineer. I want a [Sigma / Splunk SPL / KQL / Elastic / YARA] rule for the following behavior: Behavior: [describe] Data source: [e.g. Windows Security log, Sysmon, EDR telemetry, web proxy] Known noise / expected false positives: [describe] Produce:
>
> 1. The rule itself, with comments explaining each condition.
> 2. Two or three tuning options to reduce noise (with the trade-off in detection coverage).
> 3. A list of test cases (positive and negative) I should validate the rule against before deploying.
> 4. Suggested fields to add as enrichment in the alert payload to speed up triage.
> 5. Any limitations of this rule that an analyst should know about (what it would and would not catch).

Practice Exercises

First, take a real but redacted log sample from your environment and run it through the log triage helper prompt; compare its top hypothesis to your own. Second, take a benign but obfuscated string (such as a base64-encoded poem) and run the decoder prompt to build muscle memory. Third, draft one new detection rule using the rule drafter prompt and present it to your team for review.

Chapter 11

AI for Threat Hunting, Phishing, and Incident Response

Scenario: Was That Email Real?

It is 11:14 a.m. on a Wednesday. The finance team has forwarded a suspicious email to the security mailbox. It looks like it is from the CEO, asking for an urgent wire transfer. The grammar is fine. The display name matches. Only the underlying email address is slightly off. Two years ago, identifying this would have taken methodical header analysis and several manual lookups. Today, an analyst can paste the headers and body into an assistant for a structured first read, while still doing the authoritative checks in proper tools. The answer is faster. The discipline must remain the same.

Phishing Triage

> 🚨 **Phishing Email Analyzer**
>
> Below is a suspicious email reported by an end user. I have already saved the original .eml file in our case management system; the headers and body below are for analysis. Headers: [paste, with internal recipient redacted] Body: [paste, with any links shown as defanged hxxps://example[.]com style if possible] Attachments described as: [list types, e.g. one PDF, one HTML] Produce:
>
> 1. A clear verdict at the top: likely phishing / likely benign / inconclusive, with confidence (low/medium/high) and the strongest single reason.
> 2. A header analysis: SPF, DKIM, DMARC results from the Authentication-Results header; sender mismatch between From and Return-Path; suspicious Received chain; any time anomalies.
> 3. Body indicators: urgency cues, authority cues, mismatch between displayed and actual links, unusual requests, atypical phrasing.
> 4. List of indicators of compromise to extract, with type (URL/domain/IP/hash/email).
> 5. Recommended actions for the user, the security team, and the email security platform. Do not fetch any URLs. If something is missing or ambiguous, list what additional data would change your verdict.

User-Awareness Communications

Phishing analysis is half the work; communicating clearly to the affected user and to the wider organization is the other half. AI assistants make these messages markedly better, faster.

> **Phishing Awareness Note**
>
> Draft a short, friendly internal email to all employees about a recent phishing attempt that we observed and blocked. The goal is to: - Thank the colleague who reported it (without naming them) - Briefly describe the lure pattern in non-technical language - Explain the two or three telltale signs they should watch for - Reinforce how to report future suspicious emails (link to our reporting button or address) - Keep it positive and educational, not blame-y Length about 200 words. Plain English. Include a one-line subject.

Threat Hunting Hypotheses

Threat hunting is hypothesis-driven. The bottleneck for many teams is generating good hypotheses, not running queries. AI assistants can be a useful sparring partner for hypothesis generation, especially when seeded with your environment's specifics.

> **Threat Hunt Hypothesis Generator**
>
> Our environment is [brief description: industry, size, key technologies, top crown-jewel assets]. The threat actor type we are most concerned about today is [e.g. financially motivated ransomware operators, state-aligned espionage]. Generate 10 hunt hypotheses we could pursue this quarter, each containing:
>
> 1. The hypothesis in one sentence (e.g. 'Adversary establishes persistence via scheduled tasks created from unusual parent processes').
> 2. The MITRE ATT&CK technique it maps to (state if you are unsure).
> 3. The data sources required (be specific about log types and fields).
> 4. A concrete query approach (described, not full code) for our SIEM.
> 5. Common false-positive sources we should expect. Rank the 10 by likely return on investigative time, given our profile. Avoid generic advice; be specific.

Incident Response Communications

Incidents bring out the worst in writing. People are stressed, time is short, audiences are demanding, and the stakes are high. The same prompts you used for ordinary status reports become rescue lines during an incident.

Incident Status Update

```
I am writing an incident status update at [time] during an active investigation. Facts confirmed so far: [list] Facts still under investigation: [list] Actions taken: [list] Next planned actions: [list] Draft three versions of the status update:
1. For the executive sponsor (about 120 words, clear, calm, no jargon, what is known, what is being done, when next update).
2. For the technical bridge channel (about 200 words, more detail, action ownership, asks).
3. For the customer-facing comms team (about 150 words, factual but careful, fit-for-public-statement basis). No speculation. Anything not confirmed must be labelled as such. End each version with the time of the next update.
```

Post-Incident Review

After an incident closes, a post-incident review captures lessons. AI assistants are excellent at the structural work: organizing the timeline, classifying contributing factors, and suggesting actions in a recognized framework.

Post-Incident Review Drafter

```
Below is the rough timeline and analyst notes from an incident. Produce a clean post-incident review with the following sections: - Summary (5 sentences: what happened, when, impact, root cause in plain words, current state) - Detailed timeline (chronological table: time, event, actor) - Detection: how was the incident first detected, and what could have detected it earlier? - Response: what went well, what slowed us down - Root cause and contributing factors - Customer / business impact - Action items in a table (Owner, Action, Type [Detect / Respond / Prevent], Due) - Lessons learned, written without blame Follow a blameless tone throughout. If any timeline gaps exist, list them at the end as 'Open questions for follow-up'. Notes: [paste]
```

Practice Exercises

First, take a sample phishing email (your team's archive likely has many) and run it through the phishing analyzer; check whether the verdict matches your own analysis. Second, generate threat-hunt hypotheses for your environment and pick one to actually run this month. Third, for the next incident your team handles, draft the post-incident review using the prompt above and compare its structure with what you would have produced manually.

Chapter 12

AI for GRC, Audit, and Security Awareness

Scenario: The Vendor Questionnaire That Came at the Worst Time

Arjun, a GRC analyst, opens his email on a Monday morning to find a 280-question security questionnaire from a major prospect. The deal closes Friday. Two years ago, this would have meant a week of cross-team chasing. Today, with the right setup, half the questionnaire is drafted before lunch, every answer linked to an authoritative internal control or policy, and the remaining items routed cleanly to the people who own them.

Why GRC Benefits Most From AI

Governance, risk, and compliance work is heavy on reading and writing: policies, standards, controls, audits, questionnaires, evidence, and reports. The raw material is structured. The audience is demanding. The deadlines are inflexible. This combination makes GRC one of the highest-value places to apply AI assistants, especially NotebookLM, which can ground answers in your actual policy documents.

Drafting Policies and Standards

```
◐ Security Policy Drafter
Act as a security policy author for a [size and industry] organization.
Draft a [policy name, e.g. Acceptable Use Policy] aligned with
[framework, e.g. ISO/IEC 27001, NIST CSF, SOC 2]. The policy should
include: - Purpose and scope - Roles and responsibilities - Specific
rules (use clear, testable statements: 'must', 'must not', 'should')
- Exceptions process - Enforcement - Review cycle - Related documents
Write for an audience of all employees, not just technical staff.
Avoid filler. About 800 words. After the draft, list five questions
where my organization's specifics would change the wording.
```

> ⚠ **WARNING**
>
> AI-generated policies are starting points, not final documents. They must be reviewed by legal, HR, and the relevant business owners before publication. They must reflect your actual operations, not generic best practice. A policy that is unevenly enforced is worse than no policy at all.

Mapping Controls to Frameworks

If your organization is pursuing or maintaining certifications, you spend a lot of time mapping internal controls to external frameworks. AI assistants can speed this up dramatically when given clear input about both sides.

> **Control Mapping Helper**
>
> Below is one of our internal controls. Produce a mapping of this control to the following frameworks: [list, e.g. ISO/IEC 27001 Annex A, NIST CSF, SOC 2, PCI DSS v4]. For each framework, list the specific clause/control identifiers that this internal control could be evidence for, and rate the strength of the mapping (full / partial / supporting). For partial mappings, note what additional evidence would close the gap. Finally, list any framework requirements that this control does NOT cover, so we know what other controls we still need to map. Use the latest publicly known version of each framework you have knowledge of, and explicitly state if you are uncertain about the version. Treat your output as a first draft for human review. Our control: [paste]

> **NOTE**
>
> References for control frameworks: ISO/IEC 27001 (iso.org), NIST Cybersecurity Framework (nist.gov/cyberframework), SOC 2 (aicpa.org), PCI DSS (pcisecuritystandards.org), CIS Controls (cisecurity.org). Always verify against the latest official documentation, since framework versions evolve.

Vendor Risk Questionnaires

Both sides of vendor risk benefit from AI assistance: the vendor answering, and the customer reviewing. The patterns are similar: feed the questionnaire to an assistant that has access to your authoritative documents (policies, control evidence, prior responses) and let it draft answers that you then review.

Vendor Questionnaire Responder

```
Below is a vendor security questionnaire. I will provide our authoritative source documents in the next message; your job is to:
1. Group the questions into themes (access management, encryption,
   availability, incident response, privacy, sub-processors, etc.).
2. For each question, draft an answer in our voice based ONLY on the
   source documents I provide. Do not invent details.
3. If a question cannot be answered from the source documents, mark it
   'NEEDS HUMAN REVIEW' with a note about what additional information
   is required and likely who owns it.
4. Flag any answer that, if read by a skeptical security reviewer,
   might raise follow-up questions. Suggest a tighter wording.
   Keep answers concise, factual, and avoid marketing language.
   Questionnaire: [paste]
```

TIP

This is a textbook NotebookLM use case. Upload your security policies, prior questionnaire responses, and certification reports as sources, then ask grounded questions. The grounding dramatically reduces the risk of fabricated answers.

Security Awareness Content

Awareness programmes lose their punch quickly. AI assistants can help you generate fresh, contextual content week after week without exhausting your training team's creativity.

> **Awareness Snippet Generator**
>
> ```
> Generate three security awareness snippets that I can post on our internal communication channel this week. Topic: [e.g. password reuse, MFA fatigue, deepfake voice scams]. Audience: all employees at a [industry] company. For each snippet: - A short, attention-grabbing title (no clickbait) - A 90-word body that explains the risk in everyday terms and gives one specific action - A simple example that is realistic for our industry - A one-line call to action Keep the tone friendly and respectful; do not condescend or shame. Vary the formats (one story-led, one Q&A, one checklist).
> ```

Practice Exercises

First, take an existing internal control and map it to two frameworks using the control mapping helper; share with your audit team. Second, take a recent vendor questionnaire and run a section through the responder prompt with NotebookLM grounded on your policy documents. Third, generate three awareness snippets and ship at least one to your organization's communication channel this week.

PART V

AI ACROSS INDUSTRIES

From students to senior professionals, from sales to healthcare: the same skills, applied to different contexts.

Chapter 13

AI for Students and Lifelong Learners

Scenario: The Night Before the Exam

Divya has an exam tomorrow on a topic she finds difficult. Her textbook is dense, her notes are incomplete, and her lecturer's slides assume she remembers something she has already forgotten. Two years ago, this would have been a long, anxious night. Today, she opens NotebookLM, uploads her lecture slides, two chapters from the textbook, and her own notes, and asks for a study guide, a quiz, and a summary at three difficulty levels. Within an hour, she has not just memorized the material; she has understood it well enough to explain it in her own words.

This is the right way to use AI as a student. Not to write the essay for you, not to take the exam for you, not to replace your thinking, but to coach you through difficult material until you can hold it in your own head. This chapter is about that craft.

Studying With NotebookLM

Of all five assistants in this book, NotebookLM is the most underused by students. It is a study tool first and a chatbot second. Upload your sources, ask grounded questions, and treat the responses as a private tutor that has read your specific material.

NotebookLM Study Plan

```
I am a student preparing for an exam on [subject]. The exam is in [number] days and lasts [duration]. The topics covered are [list]. Based ONLY on the sources I have uploaded:
1. Produce a study plan day by day, leaving the last day for revision and rest.
2. For each day, list the topic, the specific sections from the sources to review, and one focused output (summary, mind map, practice questions).
3. Identify the three topics that look most often referenced across sources, since these are likely high-yield.
4. Identify the two topics that look least covered in the sources but are in the syllabus, so I can seek extra material for them.
5. End with five 'flag' questions that test conceptual understanding, not memorization.
```

Active Recall, the Right Way

The single most well-studied learning technique is active recall: forcing yourself to retrieve information rather than re-read it. AI assistants make this trivially easy. Instead of re-reading your notes, ask the assistant to generate questions, then answer them out loud or on paper before checking.

Active Recall Quiz Generator

```
I have just read [topic] from [source]. Generate a 10-question quiz that tests my understanding at three levels: - 4 factual recall questions (definitions, terminology, key facts) - 4 conceptual questions (compare and contrast, why this matters, how it relates to [related topic]) - 2 applied questions (a short scenario where I have to use the concept) Do NOT include the answers in your initial response. After I attempt the quiz, I will paste my answers and you can mark them, explain mistakes, and suggest follow-up reading.
```

Project and Assignment Help, Without Cheating

There is a clear, ethical line between using AI to learn and using AI to misrepresent. The line is whether the final understanding is yours. Asking the assistant to explain a concept until you can re-explain it without help is learning. Asking the assistant to generate an entire assignment that you submit unchanged is not. The first will make you smarter; the second will make you weaker.

A useful test: could you defend your submission in a five-minute oral viva tomorrow? If yes, you have used the assistant well. If no, slow down and learn the material before submitting.

> 🔍 **Concept Explainer at Three Levels**
>
> Explain [concept] to me at three levels:
>
> 1. As if I were a curious twelve-year-old (use a vivid analogy).
> 2. As if I were an undergraduate student in [discipline] who has just encountered the concept (more precise, with the standard formal language).
> 3. As if I were preparing for a research-level discussion (with edge cases, common misconceptions, and connections to adjacent ideas). After the three explanations, give me three short questions whose answers would convince you that I had truly understood it.

Career Preparation

For students approaching their first jobs, AI assistants can be quietly transformational. Resume tightening, cover-letter drafting, interview preparation, salary research, and learning roadmaps are all well within their range.

> 🎤 **Mock Interview Coach**
>
> Act as a senior hiring manager interviewing me for a [role title] at a [type of company]. The job description is below. My background is [brief summary or paste resume]. Conduct a mock interview by asking me ten questions, one at a time, in a realistic order: warm-up, behavioral, technical, scenario-based, and closing questions. Wait for my answer to each before asking the next. After the tenth question, give me:
>
> 1. A scored evaluation across communication, structure, technical depth, and self-awareness.
> 2. The three answers that need the most improvement, with concrete suggestions.
> 3. The two answers that were strongest and why.
> 4. Three questions I should ask the interviewer at the end. Job description: [paste]

Practice Exercises

First, set up NotebookLM with your current course materials and run the study plan prompt for your next exam. Second, use the active recall quiz prompt for any topic you read this week and notice where your gaps are. Third, run a mock interview for a role you are aiming at and act on the feedback.

Chapter 14

AI for Sales, Marketing, HR, and Finance Teams

Sales: From Cold Outreach to Closed Deals

Sales professionals spend most of their day reading and writing: prospecting messages, follow-ups, call notes, proposals, and CRM updates. Each one of these is a clear AI assistance opportunity, with two caveats. First, personalization must remain genuine; templated AI messages are easy to spot and damage trust. Second, anything containing customer data must respect your data-handling rules. With those caveats, AI can multiply a salesperson's effective output.

```
🤝 Personalized Outreach Message
Act as a senior account executive selling [product] to [target persona] in the [industry] sector. Below is publicly available information about a specific prospect: their company description, their recent public posts or news mentions, and their job title. Draft a brief, authentic-sounding outreach message that: - Opens with a specific reference to something in the public information (not generic flattery) - Connects that to a real challenge their role typically faces - Suggests how my product addresses that, in one sentence, with a concrete metric or outcome - Closes with a low-friction call to action (a useful resource, a quick question, or a 15-minute slot) Length under 90 words. No buzzwords. Not exclamation-mark-heavy. Prospect information: [paste public info only]
```

⚠ **WARNING**

Never paste a prospect's private contact details, internal CRM notes, or any non-public information into a public AI assistant. Use only public-domain information for outreach drafts. For deeper personalisation against private data, use enterprise AI offerings with appropriate contracts.

Marketing: Campaigns, Content, and Calendars

Marketers were among the earliest professional adopters of AI assistants for a reason: the work is high-volume, language-heavy, and benefits from rapid iteration. The skill is to use AI to multiply quality, not just quantity. Generate ten variants, choose the best two, refine those by hand.

Marketing Campaign Brainstorm

Act as a senior content strategist for a [type of business]. We are launching [product/feature/event] to [target audience] in [region]. Our brand voice is [describe in 3-5 words]. Produce:

1. Three distinct campaign themes, each with a one-line concept and the audience emotion it targets.
2. For the strongest theme, produce a 4-week content calendar with specific posts/pieces per channel ([list channels, e.g. LinkedIn, X, blog, newsletter]).
3. Five headline options for the launch announcement, ranging from punchy to descriptive.
4. Three risks or sensitivities the campaign should avoid (cultural, ethical, competitive). No clichés (revolutionize, game-changer, world-class). Be specific.

HR: Hiring, Onboarding, and Internal Communication

Human resources teams handle volume and emotion in equal measure. AI assistants help most where the work is structurally repetitive: screening notes, interview question generation, onboarding checklists, policy explanations, and routine internal communications.

Job Description Sharpener

Below is a draft job description for [role title]. Sharpen it for clarity, accuracy, and inclusivity:

1. Tighten the responsibilities into 5-7 specific, outcome-focused statements.
2. Replace any vague phrases ('rockstar', 'self-starter', 'works well under pressure') with concrete behaviors we can interview for.
3. Separate genuinely required qualifications from nice-to-haves; flag any required qualifications that may unnecessarily exclude qualified candidates.
4. Suggest two skill assessments or interview signals that would predict success in this role.
5. Add an inclusive closing paragraph that does not feel boilerplate. Keep it readable and scannable. Draft: [paste]

⚠ **WARNING**

Use AI to assist HR processes, never to make final decisions about people. Hiring, performance, promotion, and dismissal decisions involve legal, ethical, and bias risks that AI cannot reliably manage. Always keep humans in the decision loop and follow your jurisdiction's employment laws.

Finance: Models, Memos, and Month-End

Finance teams produce structured outputs on tight cycles, which is exactly where AI assistants help. They are good at first drafts of variance commentary, board memos, and reconciliations. They are not yet good at being trusted with raw transactional data; treat them as writing collaborators, not bookkeepers.

> 📊 **Finance Variance Commentary**
>
> ```
> Below is a summary of [period] financial results compared to budget for [business unit]. Draft variance commentary suitable for inclusion in a CFO report. For each line item with a variance over [threshold]%: - State the variance in absolute and percentage terms - Propose 2-3 plausible drivers based on the surrounding context I provide - Recommend one follow-up question or analysis Write in formal, factual tone. About 400 words. Do not invent driver explanations that are not supported by the context. Where you are speculating, say so clearly. Results summary and context: [paste, with any sensitive identifiers removed]
> ```

Practice Exercises

First, take a real outreach email you have sent and rewrite it using the personalized outreach prompt against publicly available information about a current prospect. Second, sharpen one of your team's job descriptions with the prompt above and share with your hiring manager. Third, draft variance commentary for your most recent finance report and compare it with what was produced manually.

Chapter 15

AI for Healthcare, Education, and Legal Workflows

Three High-Stakes Domains, One Common Discipline

Healthcare administration, education, and legal practice all share a feature: mistakes have serious consequences. They also share a feature that makes AI assistants useful: they involve heavy reading and writing of structured documents. The discipline these domains require is the same one threaded through this whole book, just with the dial turned higher: AI is for first drafts, structural support, and learning aid; humans remain accountable for any decision that affects a patient, student, or client.

> ⚠ **WARNING**
>
> Throughout this chapter, AI is positioned as an aid for administrative, educational, and preparatory work, not for clinical, legal, or pedagogical decisions about specific people. Do not paste protected health information (PHI), regulated student records (such as those covered by FERPA in the United States or local equivalents), or privileged legal documents into public AI tools. Use vetted, contractually appropriate enterprise tools for any work touching such data, and always follow your jurisdiction's regulations.

Healthcare: Administration and Patient Communication

Even leaving direct clinical work aside, healthcare professionals spend an enormous amount of time on non-clinical writing: appointment reminders, insurance correspondence, patient education materials, internal protocols, training, and quality reporting. AI assistants are well-suited to all of these when used carefully.

Patient Education Material

Draft a patient information sheet about [topic, e.g. preparing for a colonoscopy, recognizing signs of dehydration in young children, what to expect during a routine cardiac stress test]. Audience: adults with average reading skills, no medical background. Length about 300 words. Tone: warm, calm, non-alarming, but factually accurate. Structure: - A short opening that respects the reader's concerns - 'What this is' (1 short paragraph) - 'What you can do' (3-5 clear bullet points) - 'When to seek help' (clear, specific signs) - 'Questions to ask your clinician' - A closing line of reassurance Do not give specific dosages or individualized medical advice. Use plain English. Replace any technical term with a simple equivalent. After the draft, list any clinical claims that should be reviewed by a clinician before publication.

Education: Lesson Plans and Student Feedback

Teachers and trainers benefit immensely from AI assistance with lesson design, differentiated materials, rubrics, and feedback. The teacher's expertise is in knowing the students and choosing what to do; the AI's contribution is in producing the structural raw materials at speed.

Lesson Plan with Differentiation

Design a [duration]-minute lesson on [topic] for [grade or level] learners. Produce:

1. Lesson objective in one student-facing sentence ('By the end of this lesson, I will be able to...').
2. A brief opening hook (3-5 minutes) that activates prior knowledge.
3. A main teaching segment with key explanations and one well-chosen example.
4. A guided practice activity with clear instructions.
5. An independent practice activity with three difficulty tiers (support, core, stretch).
6. A short formative check-for-understanding, with the success criteria.
7. A closing reflection question.
8. Three accessibility considerations (for learners with reading difficulties, with English as an additional language, and with attention differences). Plain English, no jargon, classroom-ready.

Legal: Drafting, Summarizing, and Risk Spotting

Legal professionals deal with long documents, exacting language, and consequences of error. AI assistants are powerful drafting and summarization aids in that environment, with the firm caveat that everything must be reviewed by qualified counsel before action.

> 🔍 **Contract Risk Read**
>
> Below is a [type of contract, e.g. SaaS master services agreement] that I am reviewing on behalf of [the customer / the supplier]. Produce a structured risk read with the following sections:
>
> 1. One-paragraph plain-English summary of the deal as it is currently drafted.
> 2. The five clauses most worth scrutinizing, with the specific language quoted in short snippets and the concern explained in plain English.
> 3. Any missing standard clauses I would expect for this type of contract from my side's perspective.
> 4. A list of definitions in the contract that look unusual or asymmetric.
> 5. Three negotiation positions I might propose, ordered by likely impact on risk reduction. This is for first-pass review only and not legal advice. Flag anything that you are uncertain about or that depends on jurisdiction. Contract: [paste relevant sections]

> ⚠ **WARNING**
>
> AI output on legal matters is preparatory only. Do not file, sign, send, or rely on AI-drafted legal documents without review by a qualified lawyer in the relevant jurisdiction. Statutes, case law, and procedural rules vary widely and change over time.

Practice Exercises

First, if you work in healthcare administration, draft one piece of patient-facing material using the prompt above and have a clinician review it. Second, if you teach or train, plan your next lesson using the differentiated lesson prompt and observe how students respond to the tiered practice. Third, take a non-confidential template contract and run it through the contract risk read for practice; compare the output to your own analysis.

PART VI

BECOMING AN AI-FIRST PROFESSIONAL

Ethics, personal workflow, and staying sharp as the tools keep changing.

Chapter 16

Privacy, Ethics, and Responsible AI Use at Work

Why This Chapter Comes Before the Others

Every chapter in this book has trusted you to think about privacy, ethics, and accountability as you applied the techniques. This chapter pulls those threads together. It is short and practical. It will not make you a lawyer or a philosopher, but it will give you a working set of habits that will keep you, your colleagues, and your customers safe as AI becomes a standard part of your toolkit.

The Five Hard Rules

If you remember nothing else from this chapter, remember these five rules. They are intentionally simple, and they cover most of the realistic risks an everyday professional face.

First, never paste data you would not put in a public email into a public AI assistant unless you have explicit organizational approval and the assistant is contractually appropriate for that data. This includes customer names, account numbers, contracts, source code from your employer, internal financial figures, regulated personal data (such as health, financial, or biometric data), and login credentials of any kind. The assistant may store, log, or learn from your inputs depending on its terms of service; assume the worst unless you have read the contract.

Second, treat every AI output as a draft until verified. Numbers, dates, citations, regulations, names, and quotations are particularly prone to fabrication. Verify them against authoritative sources before action.

Third, be transparent. Where it matters, tell people when AI helped you produce something. This applies especially to academic submissions, client deliverables, performance feedback, and creative attribution. The risk of being seen as deceitful far outweighs the small effort of disclosure.

Fourth, keep humans in the loop for decisions that affect people. Hiring, firing, promotions, performance reviews, customer disputes, clinical decisions, legal advice, and disciplinary actions all need human judgement and accountability. AI may inform; humans must decide and own.

Fifth, follow your organization's policy. If your employer has not yet published an AI use policy, ask. Acting in a vacuum is a recipe for friction; acting in line with policy is the easiest way to use AI freely without anxiety.

Privacy in Practice

In day-to-day work, the privacy question rarely involves obviously confidential material. It involves the grey middle: a meeting transcript, a customer email, a piece of code, a partially redacted log. The discipline that helps is to redact before you paste. Replace customer names with placeholders. Replace IP addresses, account numbers, and unique identifiers with generic stand-ins. Most prompts work just as well on redacted data, and the privacy risk drops sharply.

TIP

Build a small redaction snippet or template for your most common cases. For example, a one-click rule that replaces email addresses with [EMAIL], names with [PERSON], and internal project codenames with [PROJECT]. Three minutes of setup pays back for years.

Bias, Hallucination, and the Limits of Helpfulness

AI assistants reflect the data they were trained on, which means they can carry biases that are uneven across cultures, genders, professions, and viewpoints. They can also be too helpful, generating answers when they should be saying 'I do not know.' Both failure modes are softened by the same habit: explicitly invite the assistant to flag uncertainty, alternative interpretations, and biases.

```
? Bias and Uncertainty Probe
Now critique your previous response from the following angles:
1. Where did you make assumptions about the audience, region, gender,
   or background of the people involved? Are those assumptions
   warranted?
2. Where are you confident, and where are you uncertain? Mark your
   answer with [confident] / [moderate] / [uncertain] for each major
   claim.
3. What is one significant alternative view or interpretation you did
   not address?
4. What is the worst plausible reading of your response by a skeptical
   expert in this field? Then, revise the original response to address
   the strongest of these critiques.
```

Intellectual Property and Attribution

AI-generated text can incorporate phrases, structures, and ideas drawn from other works. As a professional, the safest practice is to treat AI output the way you would treat a smart but careless intern's draft: useful, but in need of fact-checking and originality polishing. Never present AI output verbatim as your own analysis on assignments, publications, or work that requires personal certification. When AI substantially shaped a deliverable, disclose it. Where the assistant suggests references, verify they exist before citing them, since fabricated citations are a known failure mode.

Building a Personal AI-Use Charter

Many professionals find it useful to write themselves a one-page personal AI charter: a set of rules they personally commit to following, regardless of what their employer requires. It can be as simple as a list: which tools, with which kinds of data, with what disclosure habits, and what verification steps. Put it on your desk. Read it when you are tempted to take a shortcut.

Practice Exercises

First, write your own one-page AI-use charter and put it somewhere visible. Second, take a recent prompt that included real data and rewrite it with proper redaction; observe whether the response quality changed. Third, run the bias and uncertainty probe on a recent AI-generated draft you used at work; you will likely revise something.

Chapter 17

Building Your Personal AI Workflow

Beyond One-Off Prompts

The first phase of working with AI assistants is to use them like a search engine: a question goes in, an answer comes out, and the conversation ends. The second phase, where most readers of this book are by now, is to use them in conversations: prompt, refine, iterate. The third phase, which this chapter introduces, is to build a personal workflow: a set of saved prompts, templates, and habits that compound over time and turn AI from a tool you use into a system that supports you.

The Three Layers of a Personal Workflow

Layer One: The Prompt Library

Save every prompt that has worked well for you. Tag them by use case. Keep a private notes file or a dedicated app. Within three months, you will have a library that produces near-final outputs in seconds for the recurring tasks of your role. Appendix A in this book gives you forty starter prompts; replace them with your own as you go.

Layer Two: The Source Library

If you use NotebookLM (and you should), build a small set of source notebooks that you reload regularly. Examples: a notebook for your current project's documents, a notebook for your study syllabus, a notebook for your team's policies. Treat these as living libraries that get richer over time. The investment compounds.

Layer Three: The Habit Loop

Decide on a small number of triggers that always start an AI workflow. For example: 'Whenever I receive a meeting invitation, I generate a meeting prep brief.' 'Whenever I close a ticket, I draft a knowledge article.' 'Whenever I write a long email, I run it through the audience adaptation prompt before sending.'

Once these triggers become automatic, your output quality and pace move to a new baseline.

Tooling, Lightly Held

It is easy to spend more time arranging tools than using them. Resist this. A working setup needs only a handful of pieces: one or two AI assistants you know well, NotebookLM for source-grounded work, a simple notes app for your prompt library, and a calendar discipline that protects time for real work. Anything beyond this is optional optimization. Avoid tool sprawl; depth in two assistants beats shallow use of seven.

Measuring What Matters

If you want to be honest about whether AI is actually helping, measure something. The most useful private metrics for most professionals are: time spent on the kinds of writing you used to dread, frequency of late evenings spent finishing tasks, and your own subjective energy at the end of the working day. If after a month of disciplined practice these are not improving, your prompts may be too vague, you may have chosen the wrong tool for the task, or you may be using AI for problems where it does not actually help.

TIP

Once a quarter, do a quick audit: read your last twenty prompts. Are they specific? Did you iterate? Did you verify? Did you follow your privacy rules? This 30-minute exercise will sharpen your craft more than any new tool launch.

Sharing Without Showing Off

As your skill grows, you will find yourself producing work that surprises colleagues. Resist two temptations. The first is to make a big deal of how you used AI; this often comes across as either bragging or insecurity. The second is to hide it entirely; this is unsustainable and breeds suspicion. The middle path is mundane disclosure: when AI substantially shaped something, mention it casually. When colleagues ask how you produced something so quickly, share your prompts and habits generously. The professionals who teach others tend to be the ones who keep growing themselves.

Practice Exercises

First, set up a dedicated 'Prompts' note or document and seed it with your five most-used prompts so far. Second, identify one habit loop trigger and commit to it for the next two weeks. Third, share one prompt or workflow with a colleague and offer to compare results.

Chapter 18

The Road Ahead — Staying Sharp in the Age of AI

What Will Not Change

It is tempting, when reading a book about a fast-moving field, to feel that everything is shifting under your feet. It is worth pausing on what is not. Clear thinking is not changing. Caring about the people you work with is not changing. Curiosity, integrity, and the willingness to keep learning are not changing. None of these can be replaced by an AI assistant, and all of them are amplified when paired with one. If you keep these as your foundation, you will navigate any number of tooling shifts comfortably.

What Will Keep Changing

Specific tools will keep changing. Models will get better, then plateau, then leap forward again. New companies will appear, others will fade. Pricing will move, policies will tighten or loosen, integrations will multiply. Trying to keep up with every announcement is exhausting and unnecessary. Instead, follow two or three thoughtful sources, run a small experiment with a new tool only when you have a real problem to solve with it, and trust that the underlying skills you have built in this book transfer across tools. Prompting well, thinking critically, verifying carefully, and protecting your data are timeless craft.

How to Keep Learning Without Burning Out

The single best practice this book can recommend is to keep a private 'Things I Learned' note. Once a week, jot down two or three things you learned about working with AI: a prompt that worked unexpectedly well, a failure mode you spotted, a small habit you noticed in a colleague worth borrowing. Skim this note once a month. The compounding effect over a year is remarkable, and it requires almost no effort.

Beyond personal notes, find one or two communities, in your industry or your city, where people compare notes openly. Avoid the loudest social-media voices; seek the quieter places where practitioners share what actually works. A Slack group, a small WhatsApp circle of trusted peers, a monthly meetup, an internal channel at work — any of these will outperform passive consumption of newsletters.

Beware the Two Failure Modes

Two failure modes are common among professionals as AI matures. The first is over-reliance: leaning so heavily on AI that your own muscles atrophy. You forget how to write a status update without a prompt, how to debug without an assistant, how to plan a presentation from scratch. The cure is regular unaided practice: every so often, do hard work the long way, just to keep the underlying skill alive.

The second is reactive resistance: refusing to use AI on principle, in a misguided attempt to preserve craft. This often hides a real anxiety about being replaceable, but it ends up making you slower than peers who have learned to delegate the structural work and concentrate on judgement. Use the tools. Then use the time saved to deepen your judgement, your relationships, and your understanding of your domain. Those are the parts no AI can replicate.

A Final Word to Each Reader

To the student reading this: your generation has a remarkable advantage. Treat these tools as study partners, not as substitutes for thinking. Build the deep understanding now that AI alone cannot give you. The combination of fluent AI use plus genuine expertise will be rare and valuable for the entirety of your career.

To the early-career professional: you are in the perfect place to make AI fluency one of your defining strengths. Older colleagues are wrestling with new habits; you can build the right ones from the start. Be the person on the team whose prompts and workflows colleagues quietly copy.

To the experienced professional: do not let the language of AI hype obscure what is actually happening. The shifts described in this book are real, but the foundations of your craft, your network, and your judgement are still your foundation. Add AI to that foundation, do not let it rebuild your foundation for you.

To the manager and leader: the most consequential thing you can do is to make it psychologically safe for your team to experiment with AI, share what works, and admit what does not. Lead by visibly using these tools yourself, by sharing your own prompts, and by celebrating thoughtful adoption rather than just speed.

To every reader: the world is going to keep moving, with or without you. The chapters in this book are the same handful of habits, applied to different surfaces of working life. Pick three habits. Practice them this week. Pick three more next week. In a year, you will look back at these pages and notice that the things that once seemed impressive have become merely how you work.

Thank you for spending these pages with me. Now close the book and open your AI assistant. There is a real piece of work waiting on your desk. Try a CRISP prompt. Iterate twice. See what happens. That is where the real learning starts.

Appendix A: The Starter Prompt Library

This appendix gives you forty ready-to-adapt prompts, organized by category. Replace anything in [brackets] with your own specifics. Save the ones that work for you into your personal prompt library, and treat these as a starting point, not a ceiling.

Email and Communication

1. Universal email drafter (see Chapter 4).
2. Difficult message: delayed delivery, polite refusal, or correction (see Chapter 4).
3. Audience adaptation across executive, technical, customer (see Chapter 6).
4. Pre-send sanity check: 'Critique this email as a skeptical reader of [audience]. List five things that could be misread or used against me, and suggest fixes.'
5. Tone shifter: 'Rewrite this in three tones: warmer, firmer, and shorter. Mark which works best for [audience].'
6. Translation with nuance: 'Translate this email into [language]. Preserve professional tone and any idioms you change, list at the end.'
7. Subject-line generator: 'Suggest five subject lines for this email, varying urgency, specificity, and length. Recommend one.'

Meetings and Notes

8. Meeting notes distiller (see Chapter 5).
9. Meeting preparation brief (see Chapter 5).
10. Decision memo generator (see Chapter 5).
11. Stakeholder map: 'For this initiative, identify likely stakeholders, their probable concerns, level of influence, and a one-line engagement strategy for each.'
12. After-action note: 'Based on these notes from a project review, produce a blameless what-went-well, what-to-improve, and three concrete next-quarter actions.'

Software, IT, and Cloud

13. Code explainer (see Chapter 7).
14. Debug companion (see Chapter 7).
15. Test generator (see Chapter 7).
16. Pre-PR code review (see Chapter 7).
17. Alert triage helper (see Chapter 8).
18. Helpdesk reply drafter (see Chapter 8).
19. Ticket-to-knowledge-article (see Chapter 8).
20. Operational script generator (see Chapter 8).
21. IaC explainer (see Chapter 9).
22. CI/CD pipeline summary (see Chapter 9).
23. Cloud cost reviewer (see Chapter 9).

Cybersecurity

24. Log triage helper (see Chapter 10).
25. Suspicious payload decoder (see Chapter 10).
26. Indicator first read (see Chapter 10).
27. Detection rule drafter (see Chapter 10).
28. Phishing email analyzer (see Chapter 11).
29. Phishing awareness note (see Chapter 11).
30. Threat hunt hypothesis generator (see Chapter 11).
31. Incident status update (see Chapter 11).
32. Post-incident review drafter (see Chapter 11).
33. Security policy drafter (see Chapter 12).
34. Control mapping helper (see Chapter 12).
35. Vendor questionnaire responder (see Chapter 12).
36. Awareness snippet generator (see Chapter 12).

Learning, Career, and Industry

37. NotebookLM study plan (see Chapter 13).
38. Active recall quiz generator (see Chapter 13).
39. Concept explainer at three levels (see Chapter 13).
40. Mock interview coach (see Chapter 13).

Appendix B: Glossary of Common AI Terms

Agent:	An AI system that can take a series of actions, not just produce text, often by calling tools or APIs. Agents extend assistants from advisors into doers.
Context Window:	The maximum amount of text an AI assistant can consider at once, typically measured in tokens. Longer context windows let you upload longer documents.
Fine-tuning:	Adapting a base AI model to a narrower purpose by training it further on a specific dataset.
Grounding:	Forcing an AI's answer to be based only on a specified set of source material rather than its general knowledge. NotebookLM is a grounded tool by design.
Hallucination:	A confident but fabricated answer from an AI assistant. Mitigated by verification, grounding, and explicit uncertainty prompts.
Large Language Model (LLM):	The class of AI model behind today's chat assistants. It produces text by predicting likely next pieces of text given a prompt.
Prompt:	The text instruction you give to an AI assistant. The quality of the prompt usually determines the quality of the response.
Prompt Injection:	A class of security vulnerability where untrusted content (such as a webpage or email) hides instructions designed to manipulate an AI assistant. A real risk in agent and integration scenarios.
Retrieval-Augmented Generation (RAG):	A technique that retrieves relevant documents and feeds them into the assistant as context, producing more grounded answers.
System Prompt:	A set of high-level instructions that shape how an assistant behaves throughout a conversation, often invisible to the end user.
Token:	A unit of text the model processes, roughly comparable to a syllable or short word. Pricing and context limits are typically expressed in tokens.

Appendix C: References and Further Reading

This book has been written as a practical guide; detailed technical citations are deliberately kept light to keep the text readable. The following references and resources are recommended for readers who want to go deeper, verify the latest details on tools and frameworks mentioned, or explore adjacent topics. Where third-party frameworks, research, or product names have been mentioned, ownership and trademarks belong to the respective organizations. Always consult the official sources for the most current information.

Official Product Pages

- OpenAI ChatGPT — https://chat.openai.com
- OpenAI documentation and policies — https://openai.com
- Google Gemini — https://gemini.google.com
- Google Workspace AI features — https://workspace.google.com
- Anthropic Claude — https://claude.ai
- Anthropic — https://www.anthropic.com
- xAI Grok — https://grok.x.ai
- xAI — https://x.ai
- Google NotebookLM — https://notebooklm.google.com

Cybersecurity Frameworks and Knowledge Bases

- MITRE ATT&CK — https://attack.mitre.org
- MITRE D3FEND — https://d3fend.mitre.org
- NIST Cybersecurity Framework — https://www.nist.gov/cyberframework
- NIST AI Risk Management Framework — https://www.nist.gov/itl/ai-risk-management-framework
- ISO/IEC 27001 — https://www.iso.org
- OWASP — https://owasp.org
- OWASP Top 10 for LLM Applications — https://owasp.org/www-project-top-10-for-large-language-model-applications
- CIS Controls — https://www.cisecurity.org/controls
- PCI Security Standards Council — https://www.pcisecuritystandards.org
- AICPA SOC reporting — https://www.aicpa-cima.com

Privacy and Responsible AI

- EU AI Act information — https://artificialintelligenceact.eu
- UK Information Commissioner's Office — https://ico.org.uk
- OECD AI Principles — https://oecd.ai
- Partnership on AI — https://www.partnershiponai.org

Learning Resources

- Anthropic prompt engineering guide — https://docs.anthropic.com
- OpenAI prompt engineering guide — https://platform.openai.com/docs/guides
- Google AI for educators — https://ai.google/education
- DeepLearning.AI short courses — https://www.deeplearning.ai
- Coursera AI courses — https://www.coursera.org

ATTRIBUTION NOTE: All product names, framework names, and trademarks referenced in this book belong to their respective owners. ChatGPT and OpenAI are trademarks of OpenAI. Gemini, NotebookLM, and Google Workspace are products of Google LLC. Claude is a product of Anthropic PBC. Grok is a product of xAI. Frameworks such as ISO/IEC 27001, NIST CSF, MITRE ATT&CK, OWASP guidelines, CIS Controls, PCI DSS, and SOC 2 are owned and maintained by their respective organizations. This book is independent and not endorsed by, sponsored by, or affiliated with any of these entities. Where third-party material is referenced, attribution is provided in this section. If you believe an attribution is missing or incorrect, please contact the author so it can be corrected in future editions.

READER NOTE ON CURRENCY OF INFORMATION: AI tools, their pricing, model versions, feature availability, and policies change rapidly, sometimes month to month. Specific feature claims in this book reflect the state of these tools at the time of writing. Readers are strongly encouraged to verify current details on each provider's official website before making purchasing or implementation decisions. Frameworks such as ISO/IEC 27001 and PCI DSS also evolve through regular updates; always work from the latest official version.

About the Author

This book is the work of a practitioner who has spent 19 years at the intersection of IT operations, cybersecurity, and the everyday demands of corporate life. The scenarios in these pages are drawn from real conversations, real tickets, real incidents, and real moments of being stuck on a Friday evening with a deadline and no clear way forward. The prompts are battle-tested in those same situations, refined over many iterations, and shared here so that readers do not have to learn them the hard way.

If this book helped you, the best thing you can do is to pass on what you learned to a colleague, a junior, a friend, or a family member who has been hesitant to try these tools. The skill of using AI well is not zero-sum. Every person you teach makes the wider working world a slightly less stressful, slightly more productive place. That is the only way books like this earn their keep.

Feedback, corrections, and prompt contributions for future editions are warmly welcomed. Errors and omissions are entirely the author's own.

www.ingramcontent.com/pod-product-compliance
Lightning Source LLC
LaVergne TN
LVHW101616210926
848480LV00009B/643
9798904795733